FENTANYLDEMIC
HOW WILL THE WORLD SURVIVE

BENJAMIN HOLLAND

Ordering Information:

Prime Seven Media
518 Landmann St.
Tomah City, WI 54660

Printed in the United States of America

Fentanyl is a potent synthetic opioid that has contributed to a significant increase in drug overdose deaths in the United States. Addressing the challenges associated with fentanyl and its impact on public health requires a multi-faceted approach involving various stakeholders, including government agencies, healthcare providers, law enforcement, and community organizations.

Why fentanyl is so incredibly dangerous.

Fentanyl is incredibly dangerous for several reasons:

1. Potency: Fentanyl is a highly potent synthetic opioid. It is estimated to be 50 to 100 times more potent than morphine and many times more potent than heroin. This means that even a tiny amount of fentanyl can cause an overdose, especially if it is not mixed or diluted correctly, which is a common issue with illicitly produced fentanyl.

2. Overdose risk: Due to its potency, the margin between a therapeutic dose and a lethal dose of fentanyl is very narrow. This makes it extremely easy for individuals to accidentally overdose on fentanyl, especially if they are unaware that the drug they are using has been laced with fentanyl.

3. Illicit production: Fentanyl is often illicitly manufactured and sold on the black market. It is frequently mixed with other drugs, such as heroin, cocaine, or counterfeit

prescription pills, without the user's knowledge. This dramatically increases the risk of accidental overdose, as users may not be aware that they are consuming fentanyl.

4. Respiratory depression: Like other opioids, fentanyl can cause respiratory depression, which is a slowing or stopping of breathing. This effect is hazardous at high doses and is a significant contributor to fentanyl-related fatalities.

5. Addiction potential: Fentanyl, like other opioids, has a high potential for addiction. Individuals who misuse fentanyl are at risk of developing a dependence on the drug, which can lead to continued use despite the known dangers.

Overall, fentanyl's extreme potency, high risk of overdose, illicit production and distribution, and potential for addiction make it a hazardous substance. Efforts to combat the fentanyl crisis include increasing awareness, improving access to addiction treatment, and strengthening measures to prevent illicit production and distribution.

Fentanyl is a drug that should only be used by physicians and not the people on the street who don't want to use it to get honey. It's hazardous.

Yes, that's correct. Fentanyl is a powerful synthetic opioid that is prescribed by physicians for pain management in cases of severe chronic pain or for pain management after surgery. It is not intended for recreational use, and its potency makes it extremely dangerous if misused. Fentanyl abuse can lead to overdose and death, and it has been a significant contributor to the opioid crisis in many countries. It's crucial for people to only use fentanyl under the close supervision of a qualified medical professional and never to use it for recreational purposes. If you or someone you know is struggling with substance abuse, it's essential to seek help from a healthcare professional or a support organization.

Fentanyl is lipophilic

"Lipophilic" refers to the ability of a substance to dissolve in or combine with lipids or fats. Lipophilic substances are typically non-polar and are attracted to other non-polar substances, such as fats and oils. This term is often used in pharmaceuticals and chemistry to describe the behavior of specific compounds within biological systems. Lipophilic substances can readily pass through cell membranes and are often crucial in the design and function of drugs and other bioactive molecules.

Mental health and fentanyl don't work together.

Fentanyl is a powerful synthetic opioid that is primarily used for managing severe pain, such as that experienced by cancer patients or those undergoing major surgery. It is not typically used to treat mental health conditions directly. The use of opioids like fentanyl can have significant implications for mental health.

When misused or abused, fentanyl can lead to a range of mental health issues, including addiction, depression, anxiety, and other mood disorders. Additionally, the misuse of fentanyl can have severe and potentially life-threatening effects on both physical and mental health.

It's essential for individuals struggling with mental health issues to seek appropriate and evidence-based treatments under the care of qualified healthcare professionals. If you or someone you know is struggling with mental health or substance abuse issues, it's essential to seek help from a healthcare provider or mental health professional.

Life after a Fentanyl addiction

Overcoming a Fentanyl addiction can be an incredibly challenging and life-changing process, but it is possible to build a fulfilling life in recovery. Here are some common steps and considerations for life after a Fentanyl addiction:

1. Seek Professional Help Recovery from a Fentanyl addiction often begins with seeking professional help. This can involve entering a detox program to safely manage withdrawal symptoms, followed by a treatment program such as residential rehab, outpatient therapy, or a combination of both.

2. Build a Support System - Surround yourself with supportive and understanding people who can help you through recovery challenges. This may include family, friends, support groups, or a sponsor in a 12-step program.

3. Address Underlying Issues Addiction is often linked to underlying emotional, psychological, or environmental factors. It's essential to address and work through these issues to prevent relapse. This may involve therapy, counseling, or other forms of mental health support.

4. Develop Healthy Coping Strategies: Learning new ways to cope with stress, pain, and other triggers is essential for maintaining recovery. This might involve mindfulness practices, exercise, hobbies, or other activities that bring fulfillment without using drugs.

5. Rebuild Relationships Addiction can strain or damage relationships with family and friends. Working to repair these relationships and build new, healthy connections is an integral part of life after addiction.

6. Explore Sober Living For some individuals, transitioning to a sober living environment after treatment can provide structure and support during the early stages of recovery.

7. Create a Healthy Routine A daily routine that includes healthy habits such as regular exercise, nutritious eating, and sufficient sleep can support overall well-being and stability.

8. Set Goals and Pursue Passions Rediscovering or pursuing new interests and goals can provide a sense of purpose and fulfillment. This might involve education, career aspirations, creative endeavors, or volunteer work.

9. Avoid Triggers Identifying and avoiding situations, environments, or people that may trigger cravings or temptations is crucial for preventing relapse.

10. Stay Engaged in Aftercare Continuing with aftercare programs, therapy, support groups, or other forms of ongoing support can provide accountability and guidance as you navigate life after addiction.

Remember that recovery is a personal journey, and the path to a fulfilling life after a Fentanyl addiction will vary for each individual. It's essential to be patient with yourself and seek support when needed.

Seeking support from family, friends, and counselors after a fentanyl addiction.

Support from family, friends, and counselors after a fentanyl addiction is significant for recovery. Here are some steps you might consider:

1. Open Communication: Share your struggles with close family and friends. Opening up about your addiction can

be difficult, but having a support system in place is crucial for recovery.

2. Professional Counseling: Seek a counselor or therapist specializing in addiction. They can provide you with the necessary support and guidance as you navigate through your recovery.

3. Support Groups: Consider joining a support group for individuals recovering from opioid addiction. Groups like Narcotics Anonymous (NA) or SMART Recovery can provide a sense of community and understanding as you work toward sobriety.

4. Educate Yourself: Learn as much as you can about fentanyl addiction and recovery. Understanding your challenges and the strategies for overcoming them can help you and your support network.

5. Rehabilitation Programs: If necessary, consider enrolling in a rehabilitation program. These programs can provide intensive support and therapy to help you break free from addiction.

6. Healthy Lifestyle: Changes Focus on adopting a healthy lifestyle, including regular exercise, a balanced diet, and good sleep habits. These changes can help support your recovery and improve your overall well-being.

7. Set Boundaries: Establish healthy boundaries with people who may enable your addiction or hinder your recovery. Surround yourself with individuals who are supportive of your journey toward sobriety.

Remember, recovery is a journey, and it's okay to seek support from various sources. It's essential to be patient with yourself and to celebrate each small victory along the way.

Beware of recreational drug use because everything is tainted with drugs you don't even know, such as fentanyl. There are drugs out there on the streets right now that are even more potent than fentanyl.

Yes, it's essential to be highly cautious when it comes to recreational drug use, as many substances can be tainted with dangerous and potentially lethal additives, such as fentanyl. Fentanyl is a synthetic opioid that is significantly more potent than other opioids, and even a tiny amount can cause an overdose.

Substances purchased on the street, including pills, powders, and other drugs, can be contaminated with fentanyl or other harmful substances without the user's knowledge. This can lead to unexpected and life-threatening consequences.

The best way to protect yourself from these risks is to avoid using recreational drugs altogether. If you or someone you know is struggling with substance abuse, it's essential to seek help from a medical professional or a support organization. There are resources available to help and support for those dealing with addiction.

How drugs and mental health are ruining the world.

The relationship between drugs, mental health, and their impact on society is complex and multifaceted. While it is true that substance abuse and mental health issues can have detrimental effects on individuals and communities, it is essential to approach this topic with nuance and consideration for the many factors at play.

Here are some ways in which drugs and mental health issues can contribute to challenges in society:

1. Health Impact: Substance abuse can lead to a range of health issues, including addiction, overdose, and long-term physical and mental health problems. Mental health issues such as depression, anxiety, and PTSD can also have significant impacts on an individual's well-being and quality of life.

2. Social Impact: Substance abuse and mental health issues can strain relationships with family and friends, leading to social isolation and breakdown of support networks. This can contribute to a sense of alienation and further exacerbate mental health issues.

3. Economic Impact: Substance abuse and mental health issues can have a significant economic impact on society through healthcare costs, lost productivity, and criminal justice expenses. This can place a burden on healthcare systems, social services, and the economy as a whole.

4. Crime and Violence: Substance abuse is often linked to criminal behavior, including drug-related crimes such as trafficking and possession. Additionally, individuals with untreated mental health issues may be at a higher risk of engaging in violent behavior.

5. Stigma and Discrimination: People with mental health issues or substance abuse disorders often face stigma and discrimination, which can prevent them from seeking help and support. This can perpetuate a cycle of suffering and isolation.

While it is clear that drugs and mental health issues can have negative impacts on individuals and society, it is essential to approach these issues with compassion, understanding, and a focus on prevention, treatment, and support. By addressing the root causes of substance abuse and mental health issues, providing access to quality healthcare and support services, and working to reduce stigma and discrimination, we can begin to address these challenges and create a healthier, more supportive society.

Drugs, as a whole, have ruined many lives throughout the world as a relates to mental health issues around the globe.

Drugs, both legal and illegal, can have a significant impact on mental health and can lead to a range of negative consequences for individuals and communities. Substance abuse can exacerbate or even cause mental health issues, and those with pre-existing mental health conditions may be more vulnerable to the effects of drugs.

Here are some ways in which drugs can impact mental health and contribute to the challenges faced by individuals and society:

1. Addiction: Drug addiction is a complex condition that can disrupt brain function and lead to compulsive drug seeking and use despite harmful consequences. Addiction can have a profound impact on mental health, leading to issues such as depression, anxiety, and psychosis.

2. Co-occurring Disorders: Substance abuse and mental health disorders often co-occur, meaning that individuals may struggle with both conditions simultaneously. This can complicate treatment and recovery efforts and lead to poorer outcomes if both issues are not addressed.

3. Increased Risk of Mental Health Issues: Substance abuse can increase the risk of developing mental health disorders such as depression, anxiety, and schizophrenia. Drugs can disrupt the brain's chemical balance and impact mood regulation, cognition, and behavior.

4. Social Isolation and Stigma: Individuals struggling with substance abuse and mental health issues may face social isolation, stigma, and discrimination. This can further exacerbate mental health problems and prevent individuals from seeking help and support.

5. Impact on Families and Communities: Drug abuse can strain relationships within families and communities, leading to conflict, dysfunction, and breakdown of support systems. The impact of drug abuse can ripple through communities, affecting not only the individual but also their loved ones and broader social networks.

While the impact of drugs on mental health and society is significant, it is essential to approach these issues with a comprehensive and compassionate perspective. Prevention, early intervention, access to quality treatment and support services, and destigmatization of substance abuse and mental health disorders are essential components of addressing these challenges and improving outcomes for individuals and communities worldwide.

Life After Fentanyl

Life after fentanyl addiction can be challenging, but it is possible to recover and lead a fulfilling life. Overcoming fentanyl addiction often requires a comprehensive approach that may include medical treatment, therapy, support groups, and lifestyle changes. Here are some steps that can help build a life after fentanyl addiction:

1. Seek Professional Help: It's essential to seek professional help to detox from fentanyl and manage withdrawal symptoms safely. Medical supervision during this process is crucial to ensure safety and comfort.

2. Therapy and Counseling: Therapy can help individuals address the underlying reasons for their addiction, develop coping mechanisms, and learn how to manage triggers and cravings.

3. Support Groups: Joining support groups such as Narcotics Anonymous (NA) or other recovery-focused groups can provide a sense of community and understanding. Connecting with others who have gone through similar experiences can be incredibly beneficial.

4. Lifestyle Changes: Making positive lifestyle changes, such as adopting a healthy diet, regular exercise, and engaging in meaningful activities, can help individuals in their recovery journey.

5. Avoid Triggers: Identifying and avoiding triggers that may lead to relapse is essential. This might involve distancing oneself from people or environments associated with drug use.

6. Medication-Assisted Treatment (MAT): In some cases, medication-assisted treatment can be beneficial, particularly for opioid addiction. Medications like methadone, buprenorphine, or naltrexone can be used to help manage cravings and withdrawal symptoms.

7. Rebuilding Relationships: Addiction can strain or damage relationships. Working on rebuilding trust and communication with family and friends is an essential aspect of recovery.

8. Purpose and Meaning: Finding purpose and meaning in life beyond addiction is crucial. This might involve pursuing hobbies, education, or career goals.

9. Self-Care Learning to prioritize self-care and manage stress healthily is essential for maintaining recovery.

10. Long-Term Support: Recovery is an ongoing process, and long-term support systems, such as continuous therapy or support group attendance, can be crucial for maintaining sobriety.

It's important to remember that recovery is a unique journey for each individual, and it's okay to seek help and take it one day at a time. If you or someone you know is struggling with fentanyl addiction, seeking professional help and support is the first step towards building a healthier, drug-free life.

Fentanyl, if you don't have the right recipe, you're going to kill people.

Fentanyl is a potent synthetic opioid that is used medically for pain management, especially in cases of severe pain such as advanced cancer pain. When used appropriately and under the supervision of a healthcare professional, fentanyl can be an effective medication for managing pain.

However, fentanyl is also a very potent and dangerous drug, and it can be lethal in even small amounts if misused or without the appropriate medical supervision. Illegally manufactured fentanyl, especially when mixed with other drugs, has been linked to a significant number of overdose deaths.

It's important to emphasize that the illegal production and distribution of fentanyl without the proper expertise and quality control measures can result in a hazardous product that poses significant risks to individuals who consume it. Therefore, it's crucial to stress the importance of using medications only as prescribed by a qualified healthcare professional and obtaining drugs only from legitimate and reputable sources.

Fentanyl is being added to such drugs as heroin, cocaine, methamphetamine, and many more, so if you use drugs of any kind, be very careful and be aware because that drug multiple times before fentanyl is mixed with it will kill you.

Fentanyl, a powerful synthetic opioid, has been increasingly found mixed with other drugs such as heroin, cocaine, and methamphetamine. This mixing is often done without the user's knowledge, and it can significantly increase the risk of overdose and death. Fentanyl is much stronger than many other opioids, and even a tiny amount can be fatal. Therefore, it's essential for anyone using drugs of any kind to be extremely cautious and aware of the potential presence of fentanyl.

CHAPTER 1-A

Here are some key strategies that can help in combating the fentanyl epidemic and promoting public health:

Prevention and education: Raising awareness about the dangers of fentanyl and providing education on substance abuse prevention can help reduce its demand and use. This includes targeted campaigns, school-based programs, and community outreach initiatives.

Law enforcement efforts: Strengthening law enforcement efforts to disrupt the production, distribution, and sale of illicit fentanyl is crucial. This involves targeting illicit drug trafficking networks, improving border security measures, and supporting international cooperation to combat the global opioid trade.

Access to treatment and recovery services: Enhancing access to evidence-based addiction treatment, including medication-assisted treatment (MAT), counseling, and support services, is vital for individuals struggling with fentanyl addiction. Increasing funding for treatment programs and reducing barriers to entry can help save lives and promote recovery.

Harm reduction strategies: Implementing harm reduction measures such as naloxone distribution programs, which provide opioid overdose reversal medication, can help prevent fatal overdoses and provide a second chance for individuals struggling with addiction. Safe injection sites and needle exchange programs are other harm reduction strategies that have shown promise in reducing the spread of bloodborne diseases and connecting individuals with support services.

International cooperation: Since fentanyl is often produced in illicit laboratories overseas and smuggled into the United States, international cooperation is crucial to disrupt the global supply chain. Collaboration with source countries, sharing intelligence, and supporting efforts to combat drug trafficking networks can help reduce the availability of illicit fentanyl.

It's important to note that addressing the fentanyl epidemic requires a comprehensive and coordinated approach, involving both public health and law enforcement strategies. By combining prevention, treatment, harm reduction, and international cooperation efforts, America can work towards mitigating the impact of fentanyl and promoting public health and safety. Dealers or mixing fentanyl in everything nowadays methamphetamines cocaine heroin etc... they're even changing the colors of the pills I know right now today if you go to the corner store someone will ask you do you have any blues is the new color if you're from the streets Reckitt nice as papa Smurfs because they're blue there five times the height is heroin black tar and if they don't have the recipe right it will kill you in this book I'm going to explain how to recognize and how to avoid being subjected to epidemic I've had so many friends that died I thought they were taking one thing but it was something else more to come.

Synthetic opioids versus pharmaceuticals

Synthetic opioids and pharmaceutical opioids are two categories of opioid medications that differ in their origin and manufacturing process. Here's a breakdown of the two:

Synthetic opioids:

Synthetic opioids are opioids that are chemically synthesized in a laboratory. They are designed to mimic the effects of natural opioids, such as morphine and codeine, but the synthetic manufacturing process allows for greater control over the chemical structure and potency. Examples of synthetic opioids include fentanyl, methadone, and tramadol.

Synthetic opioids are typically more potent than pharmaceutical opioids and can have a higher risk of overdose and dependence. Fentanyl, in particular, is extremely potent, with a significantly higher potency than morphine. It is often used in medical settings for severe pain management, but illicitly manufactured fentanyl poses a significant public health concern due to its involvement in opioid overdose deaths.

Pharmaceutical opioids:

Pharmaceutical opioids are opioids that are derived from natural sources, such as opium poppy plants or synthesized to mimic natural opioids. They are manufactured by pharmaceutical companies and are available with a prescription. Examples of pharmaceutical opioids include morphine, oxycodone, hydrocodone, and codeine. Pharmaceutical opioids are regulated and prescribed for pain management in various medical conditions. They are available in different formulations, including tablets, capsules, patches, and injectables. When used as directed by a healthcare professional, pharmaceutical opioids can be effective for pain relief. However, they also carry a risk of side effects, dependence, and misuse if not used appropriately.

It's important to note that both synthetic and pharmaceutical opioids can be misused, leading to addiction, overdose, and other negative consequences. Misuse of any opioid, regardless of its origin, can have serious health risks. Therefore, it is crucial to use these medications only under the supervision of a healthcare professional and follow their prescribed instructions carefully...

CHAPTER 2

Let's talk about self-medication phone people have demons inside of them that are eating them from the inside out and their only alternative is to turn to drugs I know this because I tried it before you can get high as hell when you wake up that shit still there and that's what a lot of people don't understand. And that's why they self-medicate because of those demons the best way to combat those demons is to forgive and forget I for gave a long time ago that's the only way I survived the torture and pain that my sister and I went through that's the only way I survived to be where I am today because I was broken and I'm still broken today but I fix myself to the point where I can survive no my sister on the other hand has not and she still going through all the pain and suffering that we went through being tied up with a rope around her ankles pulled over a door so we wouldn't slip and we were whipped like slaves neck it upside down and I remember I used to tell my sister pretend like you find it that's the only way they would stop and there's so much more I can understand why my sister is still broken and traumatized today is because she never for gave in this book I'm gonna talk about a lot of things that a lot of people don't know about me I want to talk about it because I think that I can help society with regards to understanding the mental health issues of drugs because that's what they are the drugs you take drugs for pain you take drugs for so many different elements but a lot of people don't understand what and when the mind is sick they don't look at that I have a book that I'm writing called "they never gave us a manual" and that Book talks about how young parents or parents. Got so wrapped in the realm of trying to be a parent but they never gave you a manual on how to be a parent and your children suffer the consequences of that endeavor it doesn't feel good I'm still broken to this day and that's why I write because I want people that are out there that went through the same things that I went through are going through the same things that I went through to let them know that there's always a light at the end of the tunnel you have to understand that you have to realize that there's a light there and a lot of people don't understand that so that's why they turn to self-medicating and they just give up on life I never gave up so there's more to come to this chapter.

CHAPTER 3

How to save our young women and men from fentanyl.

Saving young women and men from fentanyl abuse requires a collective effort involving various stakeholders, including parents, educators, healthcare providers, community organizations, and policymakers. Here are some key strategies to address the issue:

1. Education and Awareness:

Start by providing comprehensive education and awareness programs in schools, colleges, and communities. Educate young people about the risks associated with fentanyl, its Fentanyl is lipophilic, and the potential for addiction and overdose.

Utilize diverse channels to disseminate information, including workshops, presentations, online resources, and social media campaigns. Focus on debunking myths, promoting accurate information, and highlighting the consequences of fentanyl abuse.

- Involve parents and caregivers in educational initiatives, equipping them with the knowledge to recognize signs of drug abuse and engage in open conversations with their children.

2. Prevention:

Implement evidence-based prevention programs that address risk factors for substance abuse, such as peer pressure, trauma, mental health issues, and lack of positive social support. These programs should focus on building resilience, coping skills, and healthy decision-making.

Promote positive alternatives and extracurricular activities that engage young people, such as sports, arts, mentorship programs, and community service. Encourage a sense of belonging and purpose, reducing the likelihood of turning to drugs for fulfillment.

Encourage the development and enforcement of drug-free policies in schools and colleges, along with consistent monitoring and counseling services for students.

3. Access to Treatment and Support:

Increase access to addiction treatment and recovery services, including assessment, detoxification, counseling, and rehabilitation programs specialized in opioid addiction. Ensure that these services are affordable, accessible, and stigma-free.

Expand the availability of harm reduction strategies, such as naloxone distribution programs, safe injection sites, and drug-checking services. These initiatives can prevent fatal overdoses and provide opportunities for engagement with healthcare professionals.

Foster support networks and peer support programs for individuals affected by fentanyl abuse, including family and friends. Encourage participation in support groups, counseling, and aftercare programs to promote sustained recovery.

4. Collaboration and Advocacy:

Foster collaboration among various stakeholders, including government agencies, healthcare providers, community organizations, law enforcement, and educational institutions. Create partnerships to develop and implement comprehensive strategies to combat fentanyl abuse.

Advocate for policy changes that prioritize prevention, treatment, and harm reduction over punitive measures. Support legislation that addresses the root causes of substance abuse, improves access to treatment and reduces the availability of illicit fentanyl in the market.

Engage with community leaders, media outlets, and influencers to raise awareness and mobilize support for initiatives aimed at saving young people from fentanyl abuse.

5. Early Intervention and Screening:

Implement proactive screening programs in healthcare settings, schools, and community centers to identify individuals at risk of substance abuse, including fentanyl. Early detection allows for timely intervention and referral to appropriate services.

Train healthcare providers, educators, and other professionals to recognize signs and symptoms of fentanyl abuse. Encourage them to intervene promptly by providing support, resources, and referrals to treatment.

Remember, addressing fentanyl abuse requires sustained commitment and collaboration across multiple sectors. By combining prevention, education, treatment, and policy changes, we can work towards saving young women and men from the devastating effects of fentanyl.

In this new book called" Fentanyl Demic, "I want to talk about the heroin and crack epidemic that ruined so many lives. How should one get started?

CHAPTER 4

The reason why I wanted to write a book about the heroin and crack epidemic, it's important to approach the topic with sensitivity and thorough research. Here are some steps to help you get started:

1. So I wanted to understand the scope of my as it relates to addiction, I wanted to decide whether I wanted to focus solely on the heroin epidemic, the crack epidemic, or both. So, I considered both and researched the period, geographical location, and specific aspects I wanted to cover.

Conduct extensive research and Read books, academic papers, and articles on the subject to gain a comprehensive understanding of the epidemics. I was Looking for primary sources such as interviews, documentaries, and archival materials to provide firsthand accounts.

Outline my book:

In detail the outline that organized my thoughts and establishes the structure of my book. This will help me to stay focused and ensure a logical flow of information.

I looked at the historical context that would provide me with an overview of the social, economic, and political factors that contributed to the rise of epidemics. Explore the factors that made certain communities more vulnerable to drug addiction.

I also explored the impact on individuals and communities:

Highlight personal stories and experiences of those affected by the epidemics. Discuss the toll it took on families, neighborhoods, and society as a whole. Consider incorporating case studies or interviews to add depth and authenticity.

I examined the causes and consequences: Analyze the factors that led to the spread of heroin and crack, including the drug trade, poverty, unemployment, and systemic issues. Discuss the consequences, such as increased crime rates, health issues, and strained social services.

I Investigated the response and explored the efforts made by law enforcement, healthcare professionals, community organizations, and policymakers to address the epidemics. Evaluate the effectiveness of various approaches, including prevention, treatment, and harm reduction strategies.

I Provided historical context: Situate the heroin and crack epidemics within the broader history of drug addiction and the War on Drugs. Discuss how these historical factors shaped public perception, policy responses, and the criminal justice system.

I Address current perspectives: Discuss the legacy of the epidemics and their ongoing impact on society today. I Examined the lessons learned and the changes in public attitudes toward drug addiction and treatment.

Offer solutions and hope in conclusion this book I wanted to explore potential solutions to prevent future epidemics and support individuals struggling with addiction. Highlight successful interventions, policy reforms, and community initiatives that have made a positive difference. And I want Y'all to Remember to approach the topic with empathy and respect for those affected. It's crucial to handle sensitive subjects like drug addiction with care and to provide a balanced perspective that sheds light on both the individual experiences and the broader societal context... I will be starting a forum on drug abuse, so women don't lose their children to either relatives or the state and also start a program for young men to get their GED or better work.

CHAPTER 5

Drugs and peer pressure as it relates to school colleges and the community you grew up in.

Drug use and peer pressure are significant issues that can impact students in schools, colleges, and communities.

Let's discuss each aspect separately:

Drugs and Students:

Prevalence Drug abuse among students can occur in various forms, including alcohol, tobacco, marijuana, prescription drugs, and illegal substances. The prevalence of drug use can vary depending on the specific school, college, or community. Factors such as socioeconomic status, peer influence, and availability of drugs can contribute to the problem.

Risk Factors Several factors can increase the likelihood of drug abuse among students. These include a history of family drug abuse, mental health issues, lack of parental involvement, low academic achievement, and association with drug-using peers.

Consequences Drug use can negatively affect students' academic performance, mental and physical health, and overall well-being.

It can lead to increased absenteeism, poor concentration, impaired judgment, and risky behaviors. Long-term drug abuse may result in addiction, strained relationships, legal problems, and even overdose or death.

Prevention and Intervention: Schools, colleges, and communities play a crucial role in preventing and addressing drug abuse among students. Strategies may include evidence-based drug education programs, promoting a positive school environment, fostering strong relationships between students and trusted adults, implementing peer support systems, and providing counseling services. Collaboration with parents, law enforcement agencies, and local organizations is essential. Peer Pressure Definition Peer pressure refers to the influence exerted by one's peers to conform to certain behaviors, values, or attitudes. It can be both positive and negative. In the context of drugs, negative peer pressure often involves encouraging or pressuring others to engage in substance abuse.

Impact:

Peer pressure can significantly influence a student's decision to experiment with drugs. Students may feel compelled to fit in, gain acceptance, or avoid social exclusion. The desire to conform to the perceived norms of a peer group can override their judgment and lead to risky behaviors.

Resistance and Coping Strategies:

It is essential to teach students how to resist negative peer pressure effectively. Encouraging assertiveness, teaching refusal skills, promoting self-confidence, and enhancing critical thinking can empower students to make independent and healthy choices. Additionally, fostering a supportive and inclusive school and community environment can reduce the negative effects of peer pressure.

Positive Peer Influence:

Peer pressure can also be harnessed positively. Promoting positive peer influence involves recognizing and empowering students who make healthy choices and act as role models. Encouraging peer support networks, group activities, and leadership opportunities can create a positive social environment that counters negative influences.

Overall, addressing drug abuse and peer pressure requires a comprehensive approach involving education, prevention programs, supportive environments, and collaboration among schools, colleges, families, and communities.

CHAPTER 6

How to handle drugs in the workplace as it relates to Drug abuse.

Handling drugs and substance abuse in the workplace is a serious matter that requires a proactive and compassionate approach. Here are some general guidelines to address drug abuse in the workplace, including junk abuse:

Develop a Drug-Free Workplace Policy:

Establish a comprehensive drug-free workplace policy that clearly outlines the expectations, rules, and consequences regarding drug use and abuse. This policy should be communicated to all employees and strictly enforced.

Education and Awareness:

Provide education and training programs to raise awareness about the risks and consequences of drug abuse. Employees should be informed about the signs of drug abuse, how to seek help, and the resources available to them.

Drug Testing:

Implement a drug testing program that is fair, consistent, and respectful of employee rights. Drug testing should be conducted in compliance with applicable laws and regulations and should be used as a tool for deterring drug abuse and ensuring a safe work environment.

Employee Assistance Programs (EAPs):

Establish an Employee Assistance Program or partner with external resources to provide confidential counseling and support services for employees struggling with drug addiction. EAPs can help employees access treatment options and provide ongoing support during recovery...

Encourage Reporting:

Create an environment where employees feel comfortable reporting suspected drug abuse. Implement a confidential reporting system and assure employees that their concerns will be taken seriously and addressed appropriately.

Supportive Approach:

If an employee is struggling with drug abuse, approach the situation with empathy and compassion. Offer assistance and support, and encourage the employee to seek professional help. Provide information about available treatment programs and resources.

Disciplinary Actions:

Clearly define the consequences of violating the drug-free workplace policy. Consistently apply appropriate disciplinary actions, which may include warnings, suspensions, or termination, as outlined in your policy.

Workplace Accommodations:

Understand that addiction is a medical condition recognized by many laws, and in some cases, employees struggling with drug abuse may be entitled to reasonable accommodations to seek treatment or attend support meetings.

Confidentiality:

Respect the privacy and confidentiality of employees involved in drug abuse situations. Handle the information discreetly and on a need-to-know basis, ensuring compliance with applicable privacy laws.

And develop an Ongoing Evaluation Continuously assess the effectiveness of your policies, programs, and interventions. Stay updated on best practices and adapt your approach as needed to address emerging drug-related issues. It's important to note that laws and regulations regarding drug abuse in the workplace may vary by jurisdiction, so it's advisable to consult with legal professionals to ensure compliance with local laws and regulations. What can be done for people to move forward in life without self-medicating. Moving forward in life without self-medicating is an important goal for individuals who want to maintain their well-being and lead a healthy lifestyle. Here are some strategies that can help people achieve this goal. Seek professional help: If you're struggling with emotional or psychological issues, it's crucial to reach out to a mental health professional such as a therapist or counselor. They can provide guidance, support, and evidence-based treatments to help you address the root causes of your challenges.

Develop healthy coping mechanisms:

Instead of turning to self-medication, explore and adopt healthier ways to cope with stress and negative emotions. This might include engaging in physical exercise, practicing mindfulness or meditation, pursuing hobbies, journaling, or spending time with loved ones. Find activities that bring you joy and help you relax.

Connect with support networks:

Surrounding yourself with supportive and understanding individuals is crucial. Seek out friends, family members, or support groups who can offer encouragement, listen without judgment, and provide a safe space for you to share your feelings and experiences.

Establish a routine:

Creating a structured daily routine can bring stability and a sense of purpose to your life. Set goals, prioritize tasks, and allocate time for self-care activities. A well-planned routine can provide a sense of control and accomplishment, reducing the desire to self-medicate.

Practice self-care:

Taking care of your physical, emotional, and mental well-being is essential. Make sure you're getting enough sleep, eating nutritious meals, and exercising regularly. Engage in activities that bring you pleasure and relaxation, such as taking a bath, reading a book, or listening to music.

Educate yourself. Learn about the risks and consequences of self-medication. Understanding the potential harm, it can cause to your health and relationships can serve as a strong deterrent. Stay informed about healthier alternatives and evidence-based treatments available for various conditions.

Create a supportive environment Minimize your exposure to triggers that may lead to self-medication. Surround yourself with positive influences, remove substances from your surroundings, and create a living space that supports your recovery. Communicate your needs and boundaries with those close to you to ensure they understand and respect your journey. Set realistic goals: Break down your long-term goals into smaller, achievable steps. Celebrate your progress along the way, which will boost your motivation and reinforce your commitment to moving forward without self-medication. Remember, everyone's journey is unique, and recovery takes time. Be patient with yourself, and don't hesitate to seek help when you need it.

CHAPTER 7

How to handle a drug-related relationship. Handling a drug-related relationship can be challenging and can have serious implications for both individuals involved. Here are some general guidelines to consider so Educate yourself Learn about the specific drug(s) involved, their effects, and potential risks and consequences. Understanding the situation will help you approach it more effectively.

Assess your safety:

If the drug use is putting you or others in immediate danger, prioritize your safety. Remove yourself from dangerous situations and seek help from appropriate authorities if necessary.

Communicate openly:

Have an open and honest conversation with the person about your concerns. Express your feelings and observations without judgment or blame. Encourage them to share their thoughts and listen with empathy. Communication can help build understanding and trust.

Encourage professional help Suggest that the person seek professional assistance, such as a counselor, therapist, or addiction specialist. They can provide guidance, support, and treatment options tailored to the individual's needs. Set boundaries: Establish clear boundaries that you are comfortable with and communicate them to the person. Boundaries are important for your well-being and can help encourage healthier behaviors. Seek support for yourself Dealing with a drug-related relationship can be emotionally draining. Reach out to trusted friends, family members, or support groups who can provide guidance, understanding, and emotional support. Taking care of your well-being is crucial.

Avoid enabling behaviors:

Refrain from enabling the person's drug use or covering up the consequences of their actions. Enabling can perpetuate the cycle of addiction and hinder their motivation to seek help. Consider interventions: In some cases, an intervention facilitated by a professional may be necessary. An intervention involves a group of loved ones coming together to express their concerns and encourage the person to seek treatment.

Practice self-care:

Focus on self-care activities that help you manage stress and maintain your physical and mental well-being. Engage in activities you enjoy, seek therapy if needed, and prioritize healthy coping mechanisms.

Understand your limits: Recognize that you cannot control or force someone to change their behavior. Ultimately, the decision to seek help and overcome addiction lies with the individual. It is important to acknowledge your limits and know when to seek professional advice or assistance. Remember, every situation is unique, and it may be helpful to consult with a professional counselor or addiction specialist who can provide personalized guidance based on the specific circumstances you are facing.

Understanding when you need help when addicted to a drug and how to get help.

Recognizing that you need help for a drug addiction is an important step towards recovery.

Here are some signs that may indicate you need assistance:

Loss of Control:

You find it challenging to control or stop your drug use despite your best efforts.

Health Issues:

Drug use is causing physical or mental health problems, such as deteriorating physical appearance, frequent illness, anxiety, depression, or memory loss.

Neglecting Responsibilities:

Your drug use is interfering with your ability to meet your obligations at work, school, or home.

Relationship Problems: Drug use is causing conflicts with your family, friends, or significant other.

Financial Difficulties:

You are facing financial strain due to spending a significant amount of money on drugs or engaging in illegal activities to support your habit.

Legal Issues:

You have encountered legal problems, such as arrests or charges related to drug use.

If you believe you need help, there are several avenues to seek assistance.

Reach out to Supportive Individuals:

Confide in a trusted friend, family member, or mentor who can provide emotional support and guidance.

Consult a Healthcare Professional:

Schedule an appointment with a doctor, counselor, or therapist who specializes in addiction treatment. They can assess your situation, provide guidance, and refer you to appropriate resources.

Support Groups:

Join a support group such as Narcotics Anonymous (NA) or Alcoholics Anonymous (AA). These groups provide a safe environment to share experiences and receive support from others facing similar challenges.

Inpatient or Outpatient Treatment:

Depending on the severity of your addiction, you may consider inpatient or outpatient rehabilitation programs. Inpatient programs require you to reside at a treatment facility, while outpatient programs allow you to continue living at home while attending therapy sessions and support groups.

Helplines and Online Resources:

Many helplines and online platforms offer information, resources, and counseling for individuals struggling with addiction. These services can provide immediate support and help you determine the appropriate next steps.

Remember, seeking help is a courageous and vital step toward overcoming drug addiction. There are numerous professionals and support networks available to assist you on your journey to recovery.

CHAPTER 8

When dealing with a partner who is addicted to drugs.

Dealing with a partner who is addicted to drugs can be an extremely challenging and emotionally draining situation. It's important to approach the situation with care, compassion, and focus on both your partner's well-being and your own.

Here are some suggestions on how to handle a partner's drug addiction:

Educate yourself:

Learn about addiction, its causes, symptoms, and available treatment options. Understanding addiction as a disease can help you approach the situation more empathetically.

Encourage open communication:

Create a safe and non-judgmental environment where your partner feels comfortable discussing their struggles, fears, and desires for recovery. Active listening and expressing empathy can facilitate honest conversations.

Set boundaries:

Establish clear boundaries for yourself and communicate them to your partner. Boundaries can include things like refusing to enable their drug use, not tolerating abusive behavior, or specifying the consequences if the boundaries are violated.

Encourage professional help:

Suggest that your partner seek professional help from addiction specialists, therapists, or counselors. Offer to assist them in finding treatment resources and attending appointments together.

Encourage a support network:

Encourage your partner to connect with support groups, such as Narcotics Anonymous or counseling groups, where they can share their experiences with others who understand their struggles.

Take care of yourself:

It's crucial to prioritize your well-being during this difficult time. Seek support from friends, family, or therapists who can provide guidance, and consider joining support groups for partners of individuals struggling with addiction.

Avoid enabling behaviors:

While it's important to be supportive, avoid enabling your partner's addiction. This includes not making excuses for their behavior, not providing financial support for drugs, and not covering up the consequences of their actions.

Consider staging an intervention:

In severe cases where your partner is resistant to seeking help, an intervention led by a professional interventionist and supported by loved ones may be necessary. This can help demonstrate the severity of the situation and encourage your partner to accept treatment.

Accept your limitations:

Recognize that you cannot control your partner's actions or choices. Ultimately, the decision to seek help and recover must come from them. You can provide support, but the responsibility for recovery lies with the individual struggling with addiction. Be prepared for setbacks: Recovery from addiction is often a long and challenging journey with ups and downs. Be prepared for the possibility of relapses and setbacks and try to remain patient and supportive while encouraging your partner to get back on track. Also to Remember, dealing with a partner's addiction can be emotionally taxing, and it's essential to take care of your mental health throughout the process. If necessary, seek professional help or counseling to navigate your own emotions and well-being.

How to know when you are addicted to a drug. Recognizing addiction to a drug can be challenging because it often develops gradually over time. However, several signs and symptoms can indicate a drug addiction. If you or someone you know is experiencing the following, it may be an indication of drug addiction:

Cravings and intense urge**:**

You have a strong desire or compulsion to use the drug. The thought of obtaining and using the drug becomes a priority in your life.

Loss of control**:**

You find it difficult or impossible to control your drug use. You may have tried to cut down or quit but have been unsuccessful.

Increased tolerance**:

You require larger amounts of the drug to achieve the desired effect or experience the same level of intoxication as before. This occurs because your body adapts to the drug, and you need more to achieve the same effects.

Withdrawal symptoms**:

When you stop using the drug or reduce the dosage, you experience physical or psychological withdrawal symptoms. These symptoms can vary depending on the substance but may include anxiety, irritability, depression, nausea, sweating, tremors, or insomnia.

Neglecting responsibilities**:

You neglect your responsibilities at work, school, or home. Your drug use starts to interfere with your ability to fulfill obligations and maintain relationships.

Loss of interest**:

You lose interest in activities and hobbies that were once important to you. Your focus and motivation shift primarily towards obtaining and using drugs.

Continued use despite negative consequences You continue to use the drug, despite experiencing negative consequences such as health problems, relationship issues, legal troubles, or financial difficulties.

Isolation and secrecy**:

You may distance yourself from friends and family, preferring to spend time alone or with others who use drugs. You may also become secretive about your drug use and go to great lengths to hide it.

Neglecting personal hygiene**:

You may disregard your appearance and hygiene, showing a lack of care for your overall well-being.

Physical and psychological changes**:

Prolonged drug use can lead to physical changes such as weight loss, bloodshot eyes, dilated or constricted pupils, slurred speech, or a lack of coordination. You may also experience mood swings, increased anxiety or depression, memory problems, and changes in sleep patterns. It's important to note that the presence of these signs does not necessarily indicate addiction, but they can be warning signs. If you suspect that you or someone you know is struggling with drug addiction, it's crucial to seek professional help from a healthcare provider or addiction specialist. They can provide a proper assessment and guide you toward appropriate treatment options.

Understanding addictive behavior as it relates to everyday life.

Addiction behavior, in the context of everyday life, refers to patterns of behavior characterized by a compulsive engagement in a particular activity or substance despite negative consequences. It can manifest in various forms, such as substance abuse (alcohol, drugs), gambling, gaming, internet use, shopping, or even activities like eating or exercising.

Understanding addiction behavior in everyday life involves recognizing the factors that contribute to its development and maintenance. Here are some key aspects to consider:

1. Psychological Factors:

Addiction often arises from underlying psychological factors, such as stress, trauma, low self-esteem, or mental health disorders like depression or anxiety. These factors can make individuals more susceptible to seeking relief or escape through addictive behaviors.

2. Reinforcement and Reward:

Addictive behaviors provide immediate pleasure or relief, leading to a reinforcing cycle. The brain's reward system is activated, releasing neurotransmitters like dopamine, which create a sense of pleasure and reinforces the behavior, making it more likely to be repeated.

3. Habit Formation:

Over time, repetitive engagement in addictive behaviors can become deeply ingrained habits. Habits are automatic routines triggered by specific cues or environmental factors, making it difficult to break free from the behavior even when individuals consciously desire to stop.

4. Social and Environmental Influences:

Social and environmental factors play a significant role in addiction behavior. Peer pressure, social norms, family dynamics, accessibility of addictive substances or activities, and cultural influences can contribute to the initiation and maintenance of addictive behaviors.

5. Coping Mechanisms:

Addictive behaviors often serve as coping mechanisms to deal with stress, emotional pain, or life challenges. People may turn to addictive substances or activities as a means of escape, self-medication, or emotional regulation, creating a cycle of dependency.

6. Neurological Changes:

Prolonged engagement in addictive behaviors can lead to neuroadaptations in the brain. The brain's structure and function may be altered, resulting in tolerance (needing more of the substance or behavior to achieve the same effect) and withdrawal symptoms when the behavior is discontinued.

Understanding addictive behavior involves recognizing these complex factors and their interplay. It is important to approach addiction with empathy and avoid stigmatization. Treatment approaches typically involve a combination of psychological interventions, support networks, behavioral therapies, and, in some cases, medication to address underlying issues and promote recovery.

How to control an addiction as it relates to everyday life.

Controlling an addiction can be a challenging process, but with determination and the right strategies, it is possible to manage and overcome addiction in everyday life. Here are some steps you can take:

1. Acknowledge the addiction:

Recognize and accept that you have an addiction. Denial can hinder progress, so it's important to be honest with yourself.

2. Educate yourself:

Learn about addiction, its causes, and its effects. Understand the specific triggers and patterns associated with your addiction. This knowledge will empower you to make informed decisions and develop effective strategies.

3. Seek professional help:

Reach out to a healthcare professional or addiction specialist who can provide guidance and support. They can help you create an individualized plan tailored to your specific needs.

4. Build a support network:

Surround yourself with supportive and understanding people who can encourage you on your journey to recovery. This can include friends, family members, support groups, or therapists. Sharing your struggles and progress with others who have similar experiences can be incredibly beneficial.

5. Identify triggers and develop coping mechanisms:

Identify the situations, emotions, or people that trigger your addiction. Develop healthy coping mechanisms to manage stress or negative emotions, such as exercising, practicing mindfulness or deep breathing, engaging in hobbies, or seeking emotional support.

6. Make lifestyle changes:

Modify your daily routine and environment to reduce exposure to triggers. This may involve avoiding certain people or places associated with your addiction. Adopting a healthy lifestyle with regular exercise, a balanced diet, and sufficient sleep can also contribute to your overall well-being and help in managing cravings.

7. Set realistic goals:

Break down your recovery process into smaller, achievable goals. This will help you stay motivated and track your progress. Celebrate even the small victories along the way.

8. Practice self-care:

Prioritize self-care activities that promote physical, mental, and emotional well-being. Engage in activities that you enjoy and that help you relax, such as reading, taking baths, spending time in nature, or engaging in creative pursuits.

9. Develop healthy coping mechanisms:

Replace addictive behaviors with healthier alternatives. Find new hobbies or activities that bring you joy and fulfillment. Engage in activities that boost your self-esteem and provide a sense of purpose.

10. Stay positive and be patient:

Recovery is a journey that takes time. There may be setbacks along the way, but it's important to stay positive and not give up. Be patient with yourself and trust that with time and effort, you can overcome your addiction.

Remember, overcoming addiction is a personal process, and the strategies that work for one person may not work for another. It's important to find what works best for you and to seek professional help when needed. What regards lifestyle changes in family and loved ones?

Broken promises as it relates to drug addiction.

Broken promises can be a significant issue when it comes to drug addiction, both for the individuals struggling with addiction and for their loved ones. Here are a few ways broken promises may be associated with drug addiction:

1. Promises to quit or seek help:

Individuals struggling with drug addiction often make promises to themselves or to their loved ones that they will quit using drugs or seek professional help. However, addiction is a complex and challenging condition, and many people find it difficult to follow through on these promises. They may struggle with physical and psychological dependency on drugs, making it hard to break the cycle of addiction.

2. Promises to change behavior:

Drug addiction can lead to a range of negative behaviors, such as lying, stealing, or neglecting responsibilities. Addicted individuals may promise to change their behavior and make amends for their actions. However, due to the powerful grip of addiction, they may continue engaging in destructive behaviors and breaking these promises.

3. Promises of sobriety:

Maintaining long-term sobriety is often a goal for individuals in addiction recovery. They may promise themselves and others that they will stay clean and avoid relapse. Unfortunately, the nature of addiction makes relapse a common occurrence, and individuals may find themselves breaking their promises of sobriety despite their best intentions.

4. Promises of rebuilding relationships:

Addiction can strain relationships with family members, friends, and partners. Addicted individuals may make promises to repair these relationships and regain trust. However, the challenges of recovery and the impact of addiction on interpersonal dynamics can make it difficult to fulfill these promises, leading to further disappointment and broken trust.

It's important to recognize that addiction is a complex disease, and breaking promises does not necessarily indicate a lack of willpower or moral failing. Overcoming addiction often requires comprehensive support, professional treatment, and ongoing commitment. It's essential for individuals struggling with addiction and their loved ones to seek help from healthcare professionals, support groups, and addiction treatment programs to address the underlying causes of addiction and develop effective coping strategies.

Not understanding Drug addiction in of a loved one in the beginning.

When it comes to understanding drug addiction in a loved one, it's important to recognize that it can be a complex and challenging issue to comprehend, especially in the beginning stages. Here are some factors that might contribute to the difficulty:

1. Denial:

Denial is a common reaction when faced with the possibility that someone you care about has a drug addiction. You may find it hard to believe or accept that they have a problem, and you might attribute their behavior to other causes or make excuses for them.

2. Lack of knowledge:

If you have limited knowledge about drug addiction, it can be challenging to recognize the signs and symptoms. You may not be aware of the behavioral, physical, and psychological changes associated with addiction. Educating yourself about addiction can help you better understand what your loved one is going through.

3. Stigma and shame:

Society often stigmatizes individuals struggling with addiction, which can lead to shame and secrecy. Your loved one may hide their drug use, making it difficult for you to recognize the problem. Additionally, the stigma surrounding addiction may prevent you from openly discussing the issue or seeking help.

4. Manipulative behavior:

People with addiction can be skilled at manipulating others to enable their drug use. They may lie, make promises they don't keep, or engage in manipulative behaviors to protect their addiction. This can make it challenging to see through their deception and recognize the extent of the problem.

5. Emotional attachment:

If you have a close emotional bond with the person struggling with addiction, it can cloud your judgment and make it harder to accept the reality of your situation. You may have a biased perspective or be reluctant to confront them because of fear of damaging the relationship.

It's important to remember that addiction is a disease that affects the brain, and it's not a reflection of personal weakness or lack of willpower. If you suspect a loved one has a drug addiction, it's crucial to seek support from professionals, such as addiction counselors or therapists, who can provide guidance and help you navigate this challenging situation.

So in that regard this is my personal perception of that number one never try to denigrate a person that is addicted as it relates to their addiction because all you're doing is making them want to do it more I found myself calling names and it was only because I was upset when I found out how could I have not known… but all you doing is pushing them further and further away instead of having a conversation on how to remedy the problem because addiction is a disease is not something that Anyone wants to be in and as I said earlier and a few of my other books a lot of times people have demons inside that needs to be exercised and they don't need no one constantly telling them that you fucked up or why are you doing this and that pushes them further and further away so in regards to that you have to have a conversation and ask what can I do to help what can we do to remedy this problem because I know you're hurting inside and I know you're broken but how can we fix this just simple as that but don't try to denigrate and make them feel bad because you don't understand addiction and how it relates to individuals…

I have a book that's coming out first called "Breaking Free from Childhood Trauma" A lot of people out here today are still suffering from childhood trauma and that's where a lot of the alcoholism drug addictions mental health problems etc., come from so in that regard that's why I'm writing this particular book that's because The drugs that they have out there today it's only a temporary Band-Aid or relief but when you wake up the pain hurt The sorrow is still there so with that said there's always a light at the end of the tunnel if you read my first book can you imagine never give up ever give up.

How will the world survive fentanyl let's go over again what fentanyl is and then I'll explain.

Fentanyl is a potent synthetic opioid that has caused a significant increase in drug-related deaths and overdoses in recent years. To address the challenges posed by fentanyl, it is crucial to adopt a multifaceted approach that encompasses various strategies. Here are some ways the world can work towards surviving the fentanyl crisis:

1. Enhanced drug education and prevention:

Governments, healthcare organizations, and communities should focus on raising awareness about the dangers of fentanyl and other opioids. This includes educating the public about the risks of misuse, addiction, and overdose. Prevention programs should target schools, colleges, and other institutions to provide accurate information and promote healthy decision-making.

2. Strengthening law enforcement:

Authorities need to intensify efforts to disrupt the production, distribution, and sale of illicit fentanyl. This includes targeting drug traffickers, dismantling illegal laboratories, and implementing stricter penalties for those involved in the illicit drug trade. International cooperation is also essential to combat the global flow of fentanyl.

3. Access to treatment and harm reduction services:

It is crucial to expand access to evidence-based addiction treatment and harm reduction services. This includes increasing the availability of medications like methadone and buprenorphine, which can be effective in treating opioid use disorder. Harm reduction measures such as needle exchange programs, supervised consumption sites, and naloxone distribution can also save lives by preventing overdoses.

4. Improved prescription practices:

Fentanyl is sometimes misused when obtained through illicit sources, but it can also be obtained through legal prescriptions. Healthcare providers should adhere to stricter guidelines when prescribing opioids, ensuring that they are only prescribed when necessary and in appropriate doses. Regular monitoring of patients using prescription opioids can help identify potential abuse or misuse.

5. Research and innovation:

Continued research into the development of new pain management alternatives, non-opioid analgesics, and addiction treatment options is essential. Innovation in drug testing methods can aid in the detection of fentanyl and its analogs. Public and private investments in research can lead to breakthroughs that help address the fentanyl crisis.

6. International collaboration:

The fentanyl crisis is a global issue that requires international cooperation and collaboration. Countries need to share information, best practices, and resources to combat the production, trafficking, and distribution of fentanyl. Cooperation can also facilitate the sharing of expertise and resources to enhance prevention, treatment, and harm reduction efforts worldwide.

It's important to note that overcoming the fentanyl crisis will require sustained efforts over an extended period. By combining these strategies and working together, there is hope for reducing the impact of fentanyl and saving lives.

Now I want to talk about drug abuse from the beginning of time.

Drug abuse has been a part of human history for thousands of years. The use and abuse of drugs can be traced back to ancient civilizations, where various substances were used for medicinal, spiritual, and recreational purposes. Let's explore the topic from the beginning of time.

In ancient civilizations such as the Sumerians, Egyptians, and Greeks, various substances were used for their psychoactive properties. Opium, for example, was used by the Sumerians as early as 3400 BCE for its pain-relieving and sedative effects. The Egyptians used opium, as well as other substances like cannabis and mandrake, for medicinal purposes.

The use of alcohol can also be traced back to ancient times. Fermented beverages made from fruits, grains, and honey were consumed by early civilizations such as the Mesopotamians, Egyptians, and Greeks. While alcohol was often used in social and religious contexts, excessive consumption and alcohol abuse were also prevalent.

In ancient India, the Rigveda, a sacred Hindu text dating back to around 1500 BCE, mentions the use of a plant called soma, which is believed to have had psychoactive properties. The exact identity of the soma plant is still debated among scholars.

In the Americas, various indigenous cultures used psychoactive plants for ceremonial and spiritual purposes. For example, the use of peyote cactus and psilocybin mushrooms by Native American tribes has a long history that predates European colonization.

The 19th century saw the widespread use and abuse of opium in various forms, such as laudanum, which contained opium dissolved in alcohol. Opium addiction became a significant problem, particularly in China, where the Opium Wars were fought as a consequence of the British opium trade.

In the 20th century, the abuse of drugs expanded with the discovery and commercialization of new substances. The development of synthetic opioids, such as morphine and heroin, led to increased addiction rates. The early 20th century also saw the emergence of amphetamines and cocaine as popular drugs of abuse.

The illicit drug trade and drug abuse have continued to evolve and expand in modern times. The emergence of new synthetic drugs, such as methamphetamine, MDMA (ecstasy), and synthetic cannabinoids, has presented new challenges for public health and law enforcement.

It is important to note that drug abuse is a complex issue with various social, economic, and psychological factors at play. Efforts to address drug abuse have involved a combination of prevention, treatment, and harm reduction approaches. Understanding the historical context of drug abuse can help inform current strategies and interventions aimed at reducing its negative consequences... but nowadays fentanyl, heroin, methamphetamine, crack, cocaine, etc. now I want to talk about the children who have parents who are on drugs, Children who live in a household where either parents are on drugs

Children who live in a household where one or both parents are struggling with drug addiction face significant challenges and potential risks to their well-being. The situation can have a profound impact on their physical, emotional, and psychological development.

Here are some key points to consider:

1. Neglect and instability:

Parents who are addicted to drugs may prioritize obtaining and using drugs over meeting their children's basic needs. This can result in neglect, inconsistent parenting, and a lack of stability in the child's life.

2. Emotional and psychological impact:

Growing up in an environment where drug addiction is present can lead to emotional and psychological trauma for children. They may experience feelings of fear, anxiety, shame, guilt, and confusion. Witnessing drug use, violence, or other illegal activities can also have a lasting impact on their mental well-being.

3. Increased risk of abuse:

Children in households with drug addiction are at a higher risk of experiencing physical, emotional, or sexual abuse. The impaired judgment and unpredictable behavior associated with drug use can create an unsafe environment for children.

4. Educational challenges:

Living with parents who are addicted to drugs can disrupt a child's education. Frequent changes in living situations, lack of stability, and inconsistent routines can make it difficult for children to attend school regularly and perform academically.

5. Social isolation:

Children in these circumstances may feel isolated from their peers due to the stigma associated with drug addiction. They may also face difficulties in forming healthy relationships and developing social skills.

6. Increased risk of substance abuse:

Children of parents with a substance abuse problem are at a higher risk of developing their substance abuse issues later in life. Growing up in an environment where drug use is normalized can influence their attitudes and behaviors around substance abuse.

It is important to recognize the severity of this situation and prioritize the safety and well-being of the children involved. If you know of a child living in such a household, it is crucial to report the situation to the appropriate child protective services or local authorities, who can intervene and provide support to safeguard the child's welfare.

How drugs affect relationships.

Drug use can have a significant impact on relationships, both romantic and otherwise. The effects can vary depending on the specific drugs involved, patterns of use, and the individuals involved. Here are some ways in which drugs can affect relationships:

1. Trust and Communication:

Drug use can erode trust between individuals. It can lead to dishonesty, secretive behavior, and broken promises. When one person in a relationship is using drugs, it can be challenging to communicate openly and honestly, leading to strain and misunderstandings.

2. Emotional and Behavioral Changes:

Drugs can alter a person's mood, behavior, and personality. Substance abuse may lead to irritability, aggression, mood swings, and unpredictable behavior. This can create tension and conflict within relationships, as the non-using partner may struggle to understand or cope with these changes.

3. Neglect and Priorities:

Addiction often becomes the central focus of a person's life, causing them to neglect their responsibilities and relationships. Drug use can lead to a loss of interest in activities previously enjoyed, reduced motivation, and neglect of personal and relationship goals. This can leave the non-using partner feeling neglected, unimportant, and emotionally disconnected.

4. Financial Strain:

Substance abuse can be expensive, leading to financial strain on relationships. Money that could be used for shared goals or necessities may be diverted to support the addiction. This can lead to conflicts over finances, inability to meet financial obligations, and overall instability within the relationship.

5. Codependency:

In some cases, the non-using partner may develop codependent behaviors, enabling the drug use of their partner. Codependency often involves a cycle of enabling, rescuing, and controlling behaviors that can be detrimental to both individuals. This dynamic can be challenging to break and may perpetuate drug use and relational dysfunction.

6. Physical and Mental Health Consequences:

Substance abuse can have significant physical and mental health consequences, which can strain relationships. Drug use may lead to health issues, including impaired judgment, memory problems, reduced sex drive, and increased risk-taking behavior. These effects can impact intimacy, emotional connection, and overall relationship satisfaction.

7. Social Isolation:

Drug use can lead to social isolation as individuals may prioritize their drug use over social interactions and withdraw from friends, family, and community. This isolation can lead to a breakdown in support networks and strain relationships with loved ones who may feel abandoned or unsupported.

It's important to note that not all relationships are affected in the same way, and the impact of drug use can vary depending on the specific circumstances. However, in general, drug use can place a significant strain on relationships, often leading to conflict, breakdowns in trust, and emotional disconnection. Seeking professional help, such as counseling or therapy, can be beneficial for individuals and couples struggling with the effects of drug use on their relationships.

Red flags that show your partner might be on drugs.

It's wet important to approach the topic of drug use with sensitivity and avoid making assumptions based solely on red flags. However, if you suspect that your partner may be using drugs, here are some potential signs or red flags to be aware of:

1. Drastic changes in behavior:

If your partner's behavior has significantly changed, such as becoming more secretive, withdrawn, or erratic, it could potentially indicate drug use.

2. Physical signs:

Look for physical changes that may be associated with drug use, such as bloodshot eyes, dilated or constricted pupils, unexplained weight loss or gain, frequent nosebleeds (if they snort drugs), or track marks or bruises on their arms (if they inject drugs).

3. Financial difficulties:

Drug use can be an expensive habit, so if your partner is experiencing sudden financial issues, borrowing money frequently, or displaying unexplained expenses, it could be a red flag.

4. Neglected responsibilities:

Drug use can often lead to a lack of interest in previously enjoyed activities, neglecting responsibilities at work, school, or home, and a decline in personal hygiene and grooming.

5. Changes in social circle:

If your partner suddenly starts spending time with a new group of friends who engage in drug use, it may be a cause for concern.

6. Mood swings and emotional instability:

Drug use can affect a person's emotional state, leading to frequent mood swings, agitation, irritability, or uncharacteristic outbursts.

7. Physical and psychological dependence:

If your partner becomes increasingly dependent on a substance, experiences withdrawal symptoms when attempting to quit or cut back, or shows signs of cravings, it may indicate a substance use disorder.

It's important to remember that these signs are not definitive proof of drug use, and they may also be indicators of other issues. If you suspect your partner may be using drugs, it's crucial to approach the situation with empathy and open communication. Encouraging them to seek professional help and offering your support can be valuable steps toward addressing the issue.

If you suspect that your child is on drugs this is what to look for.

If you suspect that your child may be using drugs, it's important to approach the situation with care and seek appropriate help. While no single sign can confirm drug use, several behavioral, physical, and psychological changes could indicate drug abuse. Here are some common signs to look for:

1. Physical changes:

Look for sudden changes in your child's physical appearance, such as bloodshot eyes, dilated or constricted pupils, unexplained weight loss or gain, impaired coordination, slurred speech, or unusual smells on their breath, body, or clothing.

2. Behavioral changes:

Keep an eye out for significant changes in your child's behavior, including increased secrecy, withdrawal from family and friends, loss of interest in activities they once enjoyed, declining academic performance, frequent tardiness or absence from school, sudden changes in peer groups, unexplained financial problems, or stealing money or valuables from home.

3. Emotional and psychological changes:

Drug use can impact a person's mood and mental state. Watch for signs like sudden mood swings, irritability, aggression, anxiety, depression, paranoia, lack of motivation, or a general loss of interest in personal hygiene and appearance.

4. Neglected responsibilities:

If your child starts neglecting their responsibilities at home, school, or work, it could be a sign of drug use. This might include skipping classes, neglecting homework or chores, or frequently missing work or important appointments.

5. Changes in sleep patterns:

Look for significant changes in your child's sleep patterns, such as insomnia or excessive sleepiness. Drug use can disrupt normal sleep routines.

6. Drug paraphernalia:

Keep an eye out for drug paraphernalia, such as pipes, needles, small plastic bags, rolled-up dollar bills, burnt spoons, or unusual containers, in your child's belongings or personal space.

If you notice any of these signs or have strong suspicions about your child's drug use, it's important to address the situation promptly and seek professional help. Approach your child with love, support, and understanding, and consider involving a healthcare professional, counselor, or addiction specialist who can guide you through the process of intervention, assessment, and treatment.

When you decide that you're tired of self-medicating using drugs or alcohol here are some places to get help.

Deciding to seek help for substance abuse and addiction is a crucial step towards recovery. There are numerous resources available to support individuals who want to overcome their reliance on drugs or alcohol. Here are some places you can turn to for assistance:

1. Rehabilitation Centers:

Inpatient or outpatient rehabilitation centers provide professional treatment programs tailored to your specific needs. These programs typically include medical detoxification, therapy sessions, counseling, and aftercare support.

2. Support Groups:

Support groups like Alcoholics Anonymous (AA) and Narcotics Anonymous (NA) offer a safe and supportive environment where you can share your experiences and receive guidance from others who have faced similar challenges.

3. Counseling and Therapy:

Individual counseling or therapy sessions with addiction specialists can help you explore the underlying causes of your addiction, develop coping mechanisms, and maintain long-term recovery.

4. Helplines:

Helplines such as the **Substance Abuse and Mental Health Services Administration (SAMHSA) National Helpline (1-800-662-HELP)** and local crisis hotlines can provide immediate assistance, guidance, and referrals to local treatment centers and support services.

5. Online Resources:

Numerous online resources, forums, and communities exist to support individuals in their recovery journey. Websites like the **National Institute on Drug Abuse (NIDA)** and the **Substance Abuse and Mental Health Services Administration (SAMHSA)** offer information, treatment locators, and educational materials.

6. Medical Professionals:

Consult with your primary care physician or a specialized addiction medicine specialist who can provide medical guidance, prescribe medications to manage withdrawal symptoms, and refer you to appropriate treatment programs.

7. Community Mental Health Centers:

Local mental health centers often offer substance abuse treatment programs, counseling services, and support groups. They can guide you toward the right resources available in your area.

8. The percentage of people that died from the overdose of heroin:

The percentage of people who have died from heroin overdose can vary by location and over time. In the United States, for example, the percentage of drug overdose deaths involving heroin has increased significantly in recent years, reaching a peak of 25% of all drug overdose deaths in 2015, according to the Centers for Disease Control and Prevention (CDC). However, it's important to note that these percentages can change as new data becomes available.

9. More than one million people have died since 1999 from a drug overdose. 1 In 2021, 106,699 drug overdose deaths occurred in the United States. The age-adjusted rate of overdose deaths increased by 14% from 2020 (28.3 per 100,000) to 2021 (32.4 per 100,000).

- Opioids—mainly synthetic opioids (other than methadone)—are currently the main driver of drug overdose deaths. Nearly 88% of opioid-involved overdose deaths involved synthetic opioids.

- Opioids were involved in 80,411 overdose deaths in 2021 (75.4% of all drug overdose deaths).

- Drug overdose deaths involving psychostimulants such as methamphetamine are increasing with and without synthetic opioid involvement.2

Opioid Overdose

Stimulant Overdose

Other Drugs

Data Sources

- **National Vital Statistics System** presents provisional counts for drug overdose deaths occurring within the 50 states and the District of Columbia. The counts represent the number of reported deaths due to drug overdose occurring in the 12-month periods ending in the month indicated. About NCHS, National Vital Statistics System.

- **CDC's WISQARS™** (Web-based Injury Statistics Query and Reporting System) is an interactive, online database that provides fatal and nonfatal injury, violent death, and cost of injury data from a variety of trusted sources.

- **CDC's WONDER** (Wide-ranging Online Data for Epidemiologic Research) is an easy-to-use, menu-driven system that makes the information resources of the CDC available to public health professionals and the public at large.

For the most current and accurate information, I recommend consulting the latest reports and statistics from reputable sources such as government health agencies or research institutions. also, you can go to the Center for Disease Control website to see a lot of information about the opioid epidemic.

When seeking help, it's essential to find a program or resource that aligns with your specific needs and preferences. Remember, you don't have to face addiction alone reaching out for support is a courageous step towards a healthier and happier life.

Fentanyl in middle school and high school Adolescents.

The use of fentanyl, a powerful synthetic opioid, among middle school and high school adolescents is a serious concern. Fentanyl is extremely potent and can be deadly even in small amounts. Its use among adolescents can lead to addiction, overdose, and death.

Parents, educators, and communities should be vigilant about educating adolescents about the dangers of fentanyl and other illicit drugs. It's important to have open and honest conversations about the risks associated with drug use and to provide support for those who may be struggling with substance abuse.

If you suspect that a young person may be using fentanyl or any other illicit substance, it's important to seek help from a qualified professional or addiction specialist as soon as possible.

Prevention, education, and early intervention are crucial in addressing the issue of fentanyl and other drug use among adolescents.

My name is **Benjamin Holland** and I'm sorry you're suffering from the demons that drove you to drugs and alcohol all that does is make it worse that's why I wrote this book and I think in my mind every day how will the world survive we will all have to work together as a village to help every one of us that are suffering from mental illness and choose drugs or alcohol god bless and stay safe 🙏 💯 🙌 🙏 👀